Dragon Knights

Presents

Dragon Knights

Written and Illustrated by
Mineko Ohkami

Volume 4

Los Angeles – Tokyo

Translator – Yuki Ichimura
English Adaptation – Stephanie Sheh
Retouch and Layout – Monalisa De Asis
Graphic Designer – Anna Kernbaum

Editor – Luis Reyes
Production Manager – Mario M. Rodriguez
Art Director – Matt Alford
VP Production – Ron Klamert
Publisher – Stuart Levy

Email: editor@TOKYOPOP.com
Come visit us online at www.TOKYOPOP.com

A 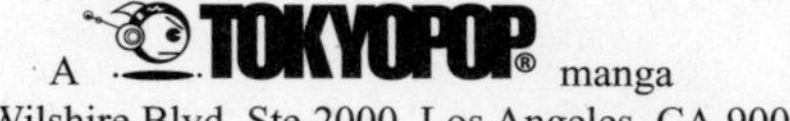 manga
5900 Wilshire Blvd. Ste 2000, Los Angeles, CA 90036

ISBN: 1-931514-43-7

First TOKYOPOP® printing: August 2002

10 9 8 7 6 5 4 3 2

Manufactured in the USA

Volume 4

The Dragon Knights in Draqueen

Thatz - Ex-thief turned Dragon Knight of Earth who has an insatiable appetite for food, drink and gold.

Rune - Dragon Knight of Water who longs to regain his Elfin powers and save his Faerie brood.

Rath Illuser - Dragon Knight of Fire who's obsessed with hunting demons.

Cesia - A Yokai, raised by a witch, whose mysterious powers are sought after by many.

Raseleane - The Dragon Queen who has been made barren by the now deceas3ed Lord Nadil.

Lykouleon - The Dragon Lord who, with his Dragon of Light, leads the Dragon Tribe.

Ruwalk - Yellow Dragon Officer and Secretary of State. Assumes command when the Lord is away.

Alfeegi - White Dragon Officer and Chief Secretary. Oversees operations in the Dragon Castle.

Kai-stern - Blue Dragon Officer and Secretary of Foreign Affairs. A close friend to Rath.

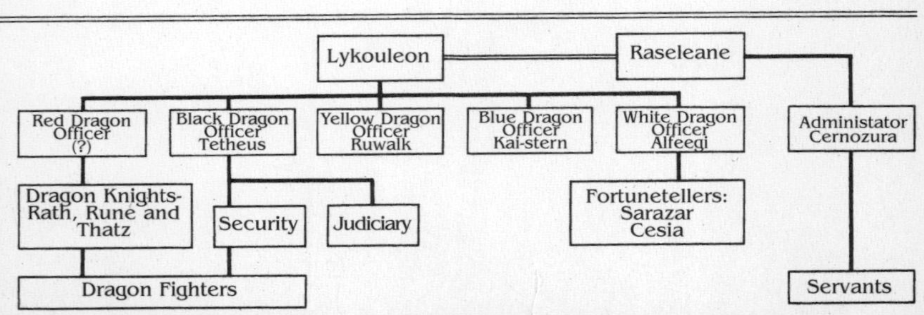

Tintlet - Elfin princess and protector of the Faerie Forest. Under Varawoo's sleep spell.

Cernozura - Dragon Castle Administrator. Attendant to Queen Raseleane and the giver of hearty meals.

Tetheus - Black Dragon Officer and Secretary of Security. A paternal force for the young Dragon Knights.

Master Kharl - A famous Yokai alchemist and sorcerer. Author of the legendary "Demon Bible."

Kitchel - Thief and former rival to Thatz. Searching for pieces of a map for the Dragon Lord.

Zoma - Yokai in love with Cesia. Unable to use his legs without the help of a magical bird.

Nadil - King of the demons who was beheaded but remains a powerful force in the realm.

Shydeman & Shyrendora - Nadil's chief officers in defacto command of the demon army.

Bierrez - Yokai in Nadil's army and the only demon who can penetrate the shield of the Dragon Castle.

Alchemist MasterKharl
- Garfakcy

Nadil
- Shydeman & Shyrendora
  - Cesia
  - Lower Demons - Bierrez and Zoma

From the Chronicles of the Dragon Knights

The Beginning: Nadil and Lord Lykouleon

When the Yokai Nadil kidnapped the Dragon Queen Raselene, The Dragon Lord Lycouleon ventured to the Demon Realm to rescue her. He defeated Nadil by cutting off his head, thereby saving Raselene, but not before the demon leader rendered her barren, unable to give Lykouleon a child... and the Dragon Kingdom an heir.

The Dragon Knights: Coming Together

Rath, part Yokai himself, unlocked the seal for the Dragon of Fire and became the first of the Dragon Knights to join the Dragon Tribe. Thatz, a human thief down on his luck, decided to steal the Dragon Rock from the Dragon Castle and inadvertently unlocked the seal for the Dragon of Earth. Rune, in a battle with the Demon Fish Varawoo, healed the Water Dragon, thereby unlocking its seal, but not without sacrificing the elfin princess Tintlet who remains in a sleep spell, keeping Varawoo contained. With Lord Lykouleon possessed of the Dragon of Light (Little Dues/Shin), only the Dragon of Wind has yet to be unlocked.

Beyond the Castle Walls: War on the Horizon

In commanders of Nadil's Demon army, Shydeman and Shyrendora had hoped to retrieve Nadil's head from the Dragon Tribe, thereby resurrecting their fallen leader. But their efforts have shifted to retrieving the Yokai Cesia who, having sought asylum in the Dragon Castle, unwittingly wields a mysterious power. The Yokai Bierrez is the only demon that has acquired the ability to penetrate the magical protective shield that Lykouleon has placed around the castle grounds, an abiltiy he has not yet revealed to his demon compatriots. Bierrez has his own agenda that involves both Rath and the coveted Cesia.

Within the Castle Walls: Strife at Home

Even with war imminent, the Dragon Tribe has internal problems to deal with. Zoma, Cesia's crippled companion, has gone missing; Rath may be dying; Rune longs to regain his elfin healing powers to rescue Tintlet and protect the Faerie Forest; and Thatz may be reunited with a past he'd probably rather forget.

Dragon Knights

Volume 4

(HOME SWEET HOME)

by

Mineko Ohkami

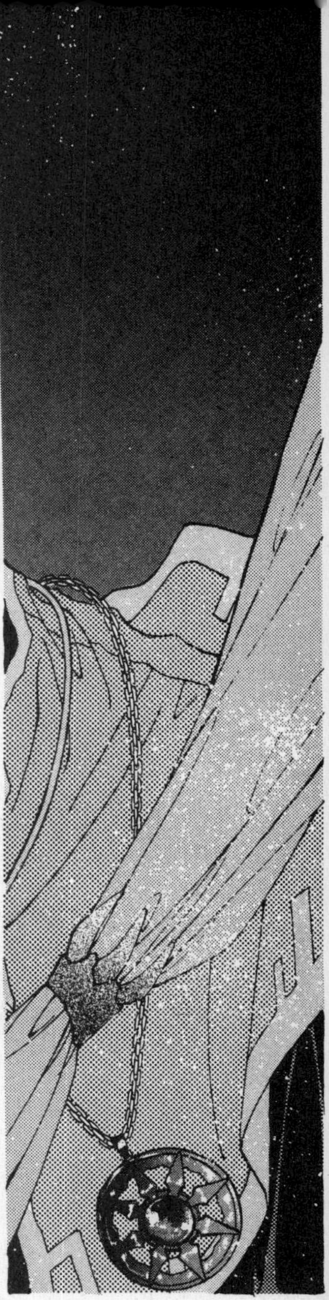

DAMN, THAT MINISTER HAS GOT THE TONGUE OF A POLITI-CIAN!

THE LAST THING HE'S THINKING ABOUT IS THE SAFETY OF ZULEBIGGIA?! GRRR!

ESPECIALLY IN THE HERMOSA PRINCIPALITY.

MY WORK IN ZULEBIGGIA IS **FINISHED**.

THAT LEAVES TWO TO GO ON THIS TOUR.
I CAN MEET WITH THEM LATER.
KAISTERN OF "BLUE"
BUT NOW...
IT'S TIME TO CAST ASIDE THE DIPLO-MAT'S QUILL...
AND GET DOWN TO SOME REAL WORK.

HERE
HMM...
THIS MAP DRAWN BY THAT GIRL AT THE HOTEL.
I'M FOLLOWING HER DIRECTIONS...
splash

BUT I DON'T UNDER-STAND THEM.
TOO abstract.
I HAD BEST ASK SOME-ONE.

SO THAT'S THE HAUNTED CAVE.
HIC THE FABLED DEN OF EVIL.

I FINALLY FOUND IT. *HIC*
DESPITE THE IMBIBING I SUFFERED TO LEARN WHERE IT IS.
Drank too much.

I HOPE THEY WERE TELLING THE TRUTH ABOUT THE DEMON.
WHERE IS IT?
ping
FAR BE IT FROM ME TO CON-SCIOUSLY SEEK A FIGHT.
BUT I NEED A...
HUH?
!!
clunk!
ponk

YEP. THAT'S A DEMON, ALRIGHT.
He sees me.

A TAD BEHIND YOUR MARK, SLOW-POKE!
CREWGER!!
OOPS.
HE'S BACK AT THE CASTLE.
Gave him back to Rath.

HIS ARMS STRETCH.

I HAVE TO STRIKE FROM BENEATH!

?!
Chtt
Chtt
Chtt
Chtt
Chtt
IT'S UNBORN-CHILDREN?!
YUCK!
THE ONLY WAY IS TO USE POISON!
flip
snpp

THAT ...
... DID THE TRICK.
....
THIS WOULD HAVE BEEN SHEER ECSTASY FOR RATH.

IT'S A SHAME I COULDN'T CARRY SOME BACK TO HIM.
Even a baby one.
WELL,
OTHERS WILL COME.

THAT'S THE SWORD THEY GAVE YOU?
WOW.
BUT IT BELONGS TO LORD LYCOULEON, RIGHT?
HE'S NOT USING IT.
AND HE SAID THAT I CAN USE IT, FOR THE TIME BEING.

ONCE, LONG AGO, I FOLLOWED HIM BEYOND THE CASTLE GROUNDS,

AND I SAW HIM WIELD THIS SWORD AGAINST A POWERFUL YOKAI.

I STILL REMEMBER IT.

NOW I CAN **REALLY** KICK SOME DEMON ASS.

rub rub

OH, GREAT.

sigh

HEY, RUNE! WHERE ARE YOU GOING?

Nice going, Rath.

What I'd do?

I'M GOING OUT.
HUH? OUT?
BUT... IT'S RAINING.
You'll get wet.
BATAN
THAT WAS STRANGE.
I WONDER WHAT HE'S THINKING.
RUNE'S UP TO SOMETHING.

sWish
NO SIGN OF BIERREZ.
RIGHT.
WHO'S THERE?!
YIKES!

YOU'RE JUST ITCHING FOR BIERREZ TO SHOW HIS FACE AGAIN, HUH?!

HMPF!

ALL MEN EVER THINK ABOUT IS BLOOD AND...

BINGO

WHAT?

THE LADY'S IN A FOUL MOOD.

OH no.
NO. ZOMA IS...
I'VE LOOKED EVERY-WHERE!
HE MUST HAVE TAKEN ZOMA.
OOPS.
shoot
Hmph

YOU KILLED HIM, DIDN'T YOU?!
NO! OF COURSE I DIDN'T KILL HIM!
WHAT DID YOU DO TO HIM?!
I DEMAND TO KNOW WHERE HE IS!
WHAT'LL I TELL HER?
IS HE THAT IMPORTANT TO YOU?
HE'S THE ONLY ONE
WHO'S EVER BOTHERED TO PROTECT ME.

.....

ARE YOU GOING TO STOP GLARING
AND TELL ME WHERE HE IS?

SUPPOSE BIERREZ DID TAKE HIM AWAY...
I SHOULDN'T EVEN BOTHER YOU WITH MY CONCERNS?!

CRACK

I SEE YOU HAVE A LOT ON YOUR MIND!

CRACK
かぱ
OW...
....

WHY DIDN'T YOU TELL HER?
BECAUSE...
I DON'T KNOW HOW TO TELL HER.
thump
thump
ZOMA'LL EXPLAIN WHEN HE COMES BACK.

LUNCH IS SERVED!
WHERE IS EVER-BODY?
I DUNNO.
RUNE!
HEY, RUNÉ!
ARE YOU DEAF!

YOOHOO! RUNE!
ARE YOU DEAD?
AHEM!
WAKE UP, YOU LAZY ELF! IT'S NOON ALREADY!
HE STILL CAN'T HEAR ME?
WELL, WHEN IN DOUBT-
...USE BRUTE FORCE.
I'll whack his head.
HEY, OGRE! CAN'T YOU SEE I'M MEDITATING?!
amateur

I WAS JUST TESTING YOUR LEVEL OF FOCUS.
I knew it all along.
....
SO,
WHY THE ZONING OUT, ANYWAY?
I'M TRYING TO REGAIN MY ELFIN POWERS.
HUH?
YOUR WHAT?
THE NATURAL POWER TO HEAL
ALL ELVES HAVE IT.

WHEN I BECAME A DRAGON KNIGHT, MY HEALING ABILITIES VANISHED.
I NEED THOSE ABILITIES TO FEEL WHOLE AS A MEMBER OF THE ELFIN RACE.
NOW, I CAN'T EVEN BLOOM A WILTED FLOWER.
MY "ZONING OUT" IS A WAY TO FIND A SOURCE FOR THIS BLOCK.
IT SOUNDS HARD.
ANY LUCK?
NOT YET, BUT I'VE LEARNED GREATER CONTROL OVER WATER.
I MADE THIS.
WHAT IS IT?
A HEAVEN'S AQUA-BALL.
IT'S ABLE TO HOLD VAST AMOUNTS OF WATER.
AND THE WATER DRAGON ALONE WON'T BE ABLE TO KEEP VARAWOO SEALED.
I NEED TO HEAL TINTLET ENOUGH TO ESCAPE THE MON-STER'S TOMB.

IT CAN COME IN HANDY ON LONG JOURNEYS.
WOW!
THAT'S COOL!
CAN I HAVE IT?
UH, SURE.
Whoopee!
IS HE GOING SOMEWHERE?
WAIT.
HOLD ON.
I JUST REMEMBERED SOMETHING.
HMM?

SOME-THING I REMEMBER THAT ELFIN FORTUNE TELLER DELTE SAYING.
ABOUT RATH.
SHE SAID HE'S DYING... REMEMBER?
MAYBE WE SHOULD TELL THE DRAGON LORD.
WE WILL. BUT NOT NOW
NOW HE NEEDS TO FOCUS ON THE YOKAI.
?!

WHAT THE HELL?!
!!

!
THATZ!

THATZ?!
THATZ?!
ugh
ANSWER ME!
THATZ!!

gasp
HUH?

RUNE, SIR!
WE'RE HERE!
HURRY UP!
THATZ NEEDS HELP!
する…

IT LOOKS BAD.
IS HE GOING TO BE OKAY?
I DON'T KNOW.

I'M BA-ACK.
JUST LIKE I PROMISED, DARLING. DISAP-POINTED?
NO. NOW I GET TO WATCH YOU DIE.
I DON'T CONSIDER THE DRAGON TRIBE MUCH OF A THREAT.
OH?
THINK NOT?
RATH WILL RIP OUT YOUR THROAT AND COOK IT FOR BREAKFAST. HE'LL STOP YOU.
COLOR-FUL, BUT TINGED WITH BLIND OPTI-MISM.
WHAT?

YOU HAVEN'T HEARD THE NEWS?
RIGHT NOW, YOUR PRECIOUS DRAGON TRIBE IS CURRENTLY ENGAGED IN FIGHTING...
...OTHER DEMONS.
IS THAT ...
... SO?
I'M NOT SO GOOD.
CLINK
I'D RATHER NOT HAVE TO USE THE RING ON YOU.
SO BE A GOOD GIRL.
IF YOU ANSWER ME ONE QUESTION, I'LL GO WITH YOU... PEACEFULLY.

BY ALL MEANS. WHAT DO YOU WANT TO KNOW?
WHY AM I SO IMPORTANT?
WHY DOES NADIL'S ARMY NEED ME?
IT'S NOT JUST NADIL'S ARMY.
YOU SEE...
YOU'RE VALUABLE TO ANYONE WHO WANTS TO UNLOCK VAST AMOUNTS OF POWER.
DEMON AND DRAGON ALIKE.
!
BECAUSE WITH YOU...
WAIT...

!?
YOU ARE NOT ...!!
WHO ARE YOU?
NOT BAD.
YOU SAW THROUGH MY DIS-GUISE.
I ONLY WISH...
...YOU WERE FOOLED LONG ENOUGH...

...TO GIVE ME THE ANSWER ....
BIERREZ.

YOU WANT THE ANS-WER?
FINE. I'LL TELL YOU.
AND THEN RIP YOUR THROAT OUT.

KNOCK
KNOCK

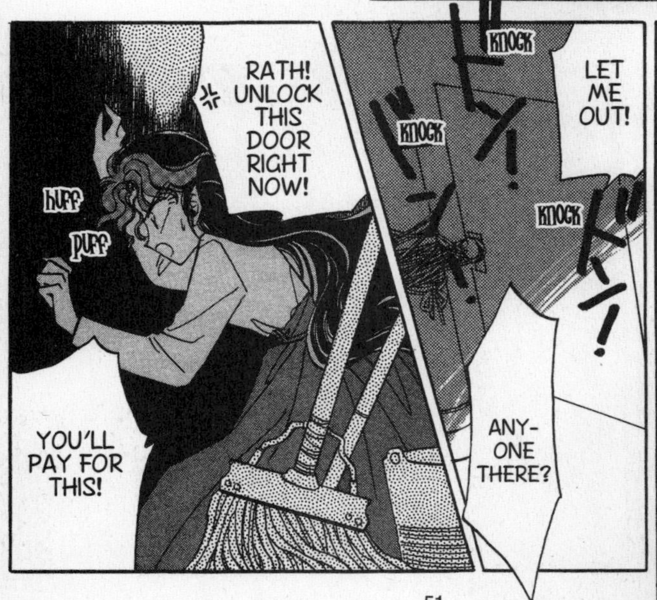
LET ME OUT!
KNOCK
KNOCK
KNOCK
ANY-ONE THERE?
RATH! UNLOCK THIS DOOR RIGHT NOW!
huff
puff
YOU'LL PAY FOR THIS!

I'M GETTING HUNGRY.
growl
was kidnapped at lunchtime
click
!
OH.
DID YOU OPEN THE DOOR?
THANK YOU.
UH...
YOU'RE RATH'S DOG. I FORGET YOUR NAME.
WELL, THANKS FOR OPENING THE DOOR.

WAIT A SEC... YOUR NAME'S CREWGER, RIGHT?
DID YOU JUST...
... TALK?
YOU CAN TALK.
CESIA'S PRESENCE...
CAN AMPLIFY POWER. ANYONE'S POWER. WITHOUT HER EVEN HAVING TO WILL IT.
A DEMON'S POWER,
OR THE DRAGON LORD'S LIGHT!
THAT'S WHY NADIL TOOK HER.
SHE WAS JUST A SCARED LITTLE CHILD.

BUT HE TRAINED HER.

TRAINED HER TO HARNESS HER ABILITY TO CONTROL THE WIND.

IT MAKES SENSE NOW.

It was her Wind.

The Wind opened Nadil's eyes in Misty Valley!

And it gave me power in Chantel!

WITH CESIA AT THE CASTLE...

THE LORD'S LIGHT MUST BE REALLY POWERFUL AGAINST DEMONS.

HA!

HE'S NOT THAT POWERFUL. DON'T SWOON... OR REST COMPLACENT.

THANKS FOR THE ANSWER I SOUGHT.
NOW IT'S EVEN MORE NECESSARY FOR ME TO KEEP ANY YOKAI FROM STEALING HER AGAIN...
I'M TAKING HER BACK!!
IF YOU WANT HER, BIERREZ...
YOU'RE GOING TO HAVE TO...
...GO THROUGH ME FIRST!

THOSE EYES!
I'M ALWAYS UP FOR A FAIR FIGHT?
CLICK
I'VE SEEN THEM BEFORE!!

YANK
THERE'S A DEMON HERE?
WHAT? IT'S NOT JUST HIM?!
THERE'RE MANY?!
IS IT BIERREZ?
PULL
OKAY. I KNOW.
THAT'S WHY I'M HERE.
CREAK

THIS IS A SAFE PLACE?
nod nod
OKAY.
THANKS.
I MUST ...
I MUST HELP THEM!

THE WITCH'S CRYSTAL BALL...

....
THIS DEMON ...
HOW MANY ARE THERE?!
HOW CAN THEY PENETRATE THE LORD'S PROTECTIVE SHIELD?

HOW MANY ARE LEFT?
TOO MANY.
THEY'RE COMING IN DROVES.
IT'S AS IF THEY'RE APPEARING MAGICALLY.
WE MAY HAVE TO EVACUATE THIS AREA.
WHERE'S THE LORD?
HE'S TRY-ING TO STREGTHEN THE SHIELD.

THIS IS THE BEST I CAN DO RIGHT NOW.
IF I HAD MY ELFIN POWERS, I COULD HEAL THATZ!
WE CAN'T LET THEM ADVANCE.
WATER!
HERE WE GO!
THE DEMONS ARE BEING GENERATED BY BIERREZ.
THEY'RE BORN OF HIS MATTER.
THEY HAVE HIS ABILITY TO RESIST THE SHIELD.

WHEN DID BIERREZ LEARN TO CREATE DEMONS?
THATZ HAS BEEN WOUNDED BADLY.
HE'S UNCON-SCIOUS.
SEVERAL DRAGON OFFICERS ARE INJURED AS WELL.
THE DEMONS ARE COMING TOO FAST.
HOW CAN WE HELP THEM,
CREWGER?

JUST DO MY BEST?
BUT AT MY BEST I CAN ONLY CONTROL WIND.
I CAN'T DO ANY OTHER MAGIC!
I CAN'T.
I DON'T KNOW HOW.
WHAT HELP COULD I POSSIBLY BE?!
MY WIND CAN ONLY GO SO FAR.
DRAGON LORD...
YOU WOULDN'T HAVE ASKED ME TO STAY IF I WERE USELESS...
BUT I'M NOT READY.
OH, RATH IS!
HE LOCKED ME IN THAT CLOSET!
はっ
grrr
AND NOW HE'S PROBABLY FIGHTING BIERREZ!
it's what he was waiting for.
nod
nod
WAIT. IF WE DEFEAT BIERREZ...

...THE DEMONS WOULD LOSE THEIR LIFE FORCE!
THEY CAN'T EXIST WITHOUT HIM!
I'LL HELP RATH BY CREATING AN ILLUSION!
THIS MIGHT JUST WORK!
WIND.

WHAT THE...?
WIND?
FOG?
!
AN ILLUSION!

A CYCLOPIAN ...
あら?
HUH?
... BEAST?
GRRRR!
Oh no!
What is that?
NOT ENTIRELY WHAT I INTENDED...
BUT NOT ENTIRELY UNEFFECTIVE.
RIGHT?
I GOT CON-FUSED.
?!

RUNE!!
HE'S CAUGHT IN THE WIND!
!
blink
THATZ, SIR! WHERE ARE YOU?

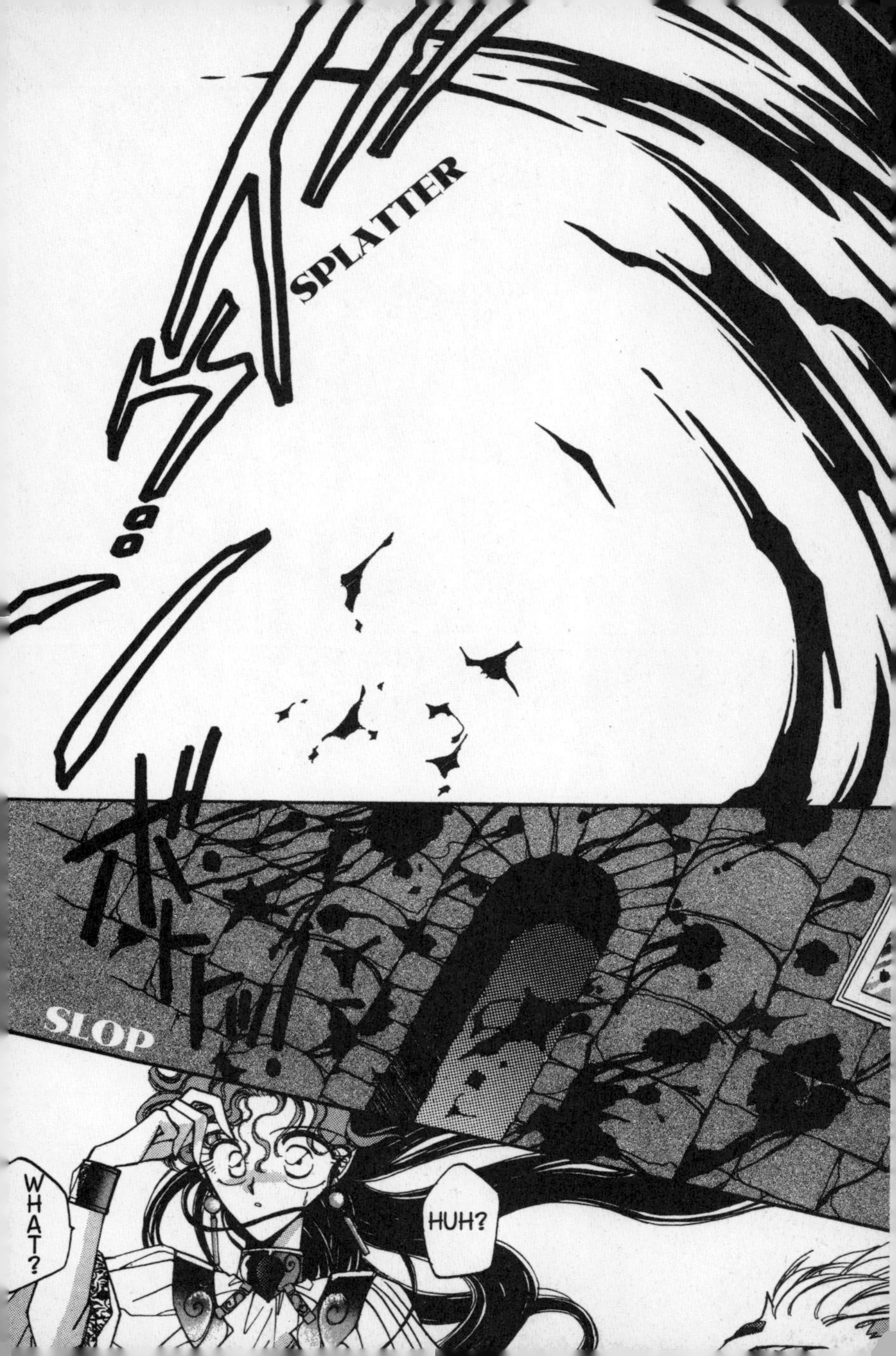

SPLATTER
SLOP
HUH?
WHAT?

IT'S BLOOD.

AND PIECES OF DEMON.

RAIN.

splash

splash

splash

シュウウウ…

WHAT HAPPENED?
flap
THE CRYSTAL BALL.

ざあっ
!
ぱしゃっ!
RUNE ...
RUNE, SIR!
WHAT HAP-PENED?
YOUR HAIR... IT'S TURNED ...
WHERE'S THATZ?
HE'S OVER THERE.

AM I ALIVE?
SIR! ARE YOU OKAY?
.....
?! HUH?
LOOK!
HIS WOUNDS HAVE HEALED!
IT LOOKS LIKE I SLEW SOME DEMONS.
I CAN'T REMEMBER...
BUT I FEEL DIFFER-ENT.
THATZ?!

THE WATER AND EARTH DRAGON KNIGHTS HAVE CHANGED FORM...
...HAVE CHANGED FORM?
THEY ARE EACH STRONGER,
MORE POWER-FUL.
BUT HOW?
I just don't get the Dragon Tribe.
MY ILLUSION SUCKED. BUT AT LEAST THEY'RE OUT OF DANGER.
I NEED TO PRACTICE MY MAGIC.

NOW, WHERE ARE YOU BIERREZ ...
OW!!
IT'LL BE OKAY.
RATH HAS FOUND HIM.
THE SAME THING HAPPENED LAST TIME,
WHEN I TRIED TO DISCOVER WHOSE GRAVE RATH VISITS.
MY SPELL FAILED.
I CAN'T EXPLAIN IT, BUT RATH IS IMMUNE TO MY MAGIC.
I CAN'T SEE HIM IN MY CRYSTAL.
I wonder why

RATH IS GOING TO HAVE TO FACE BIERREZ ALONE.
Ruwalk said the same thing
WE NEED TO REPORT WHAT WE'VE LEARNED TO THE DRAGON LORD.
MY POWERS HAVE TO BE OF USE SOMEHOW.
I HAVE TO BE USEFUL ...
SOME-HOW.

HIS ENERGY IS FAMILIAR.
IT'S UNSETTLING.
YAAAA!
HE'S NOT ENTIRELY DRAGON!
ドーオッ!!

!
と…

HATE TO BE RUDE...
BUT I DON'T EVEN KNOW WHO YOU ARE?
WHAT?

YOU DON'T REMEMBER ME...
BIERREZ?

YOU SHOULD.
THE ONLY ONES WHO KNOW WHO I TRULY AM ARE THE INNER CIRCLE OF THE DRAGON TRIBE...
...AND **YOU.**

EVERY-ONE ELSE IS DEAD.
!

I NEVER HAD A NAME...
SO THE DRAGON TRIBE GAVE ME ONE. **RATH ILLUSER.**

ILLUSER ?!
"RATH" WAS JUST SOME RANDOM MONIKER, CHOSEN BY ONE OF THE OFFICERS.
BUT YOU RECOG-NIZE THE NAME **ILLUSER.**

I REMEMBER NOW. WHEN I WAS DRAWN TO ILLUSER'S LIGHT...

... AND YOU WERE THERE.

IT WAS YOU!!

YES. IT WAS ME.

OW
...
He's too strong

DID YOU ...

CESIA!

HEAR US?

WHAT?
DON'T BAT THOSE BIG EYES AT ME!
DID YOU HEAR OR DIDN'T YOU?!

LOOK!
I'M ON MY WAY TO SEE THE DRAGON LORD!
SO, I'LL LEAVE YOU AND YOUR IMAGINARY FRIENDS TO TALK ABOUT WHATEVER?!

OH.
OKAY THEN.
I'M GONNA GO FINISH BEATING UP BIERREZ.
YOU FORGETTING SOMETHING, RATH?
NOT SO FAST.
OH, I SEE YOU GOT OUT OF THE CLOSET! GOOD FOR YOU.
GREAT.
MAYBE THEY SAVED YOU SOME LUNCH.
ONE MORE THING.
DON'T LET BIERREZ KIDNAP YOU. NOTHING WOULD ANNOY ME MORE THAN HAVING TO STAGE A RESCUE.
grrrr
NOW I'M GLAD I CAN'T SEE HIM IN MY CRYSTAL BALL!

YANK
NO...

WHAT WAS THE DRAGON LORD THINKING?!
HE GAVE IT A DRAGON NAME? AND TREATS IT LIKE ONE OF HIS OWN?!

DAMN.
I'VE FAILED!
I WAS FOOLISHLY SHORT-SIGHTED.
THAT MAN!
HE USED MASTER KHARL'S MAGIC TO MAKE DEMONS.

HEY, WAIT A SECOND.
RATH SHOULD HAVE CHANGED FORM,
LIKE THE OTHER TWO.

I KNOW WHAT YOU'RE THINKING.

huh?

WHAT?

BUT NADIL'S ARMY...

WILL NEVER GET CESIA BACK.

Ching!

Ching!

DAMN IT!
カラン…
CLIIINK
SORRY.

?
BLOCKED!!
YOU!
WHO ARE YOU?!

SOME-ONE WHO'S COME...
... FOR THIS.
?!
ASHES?!

THEY'RE GONE...

BIERREZ'LL BE BACK.
I WONDER WHO HIS NEW FRIEND IS.

THATZ? RUNE?

OH... WOW.
HA HA
cut it off
BOTH OF YOU LOOK SO DIFFERENT.
RUNE.
HAVE YOU REGAINED YOUR ELFIN POWERS AS WELL?
HM?
UH ...
YES, SIRE.

YOUR MAJESTY, HERE'S TETHEUS' REPORT ON THE BATTLE.
WHERE IS HE?
HE'S STILL SURVEYING THE BATTLE SITE, MY LORD.

AND RUNE HAS HEALED ALL THE INJURED FIGHTERS.
SO THE REPORT IS QUITE FAVORABLE..

GOOD.
HOW DID THE DEMONS GET INTO THE CASTLE IN THE FIRST PLACE?
CESIA SAID THAT THERE WAS AN ARCANE MAGIC AT WORK.
YOU LET HIM GET AWAY?!

I CAN'T BELIEVE THIS. HE STILL HAS THE ABILITY TO PENE-TRATE THE SHIELD, RIGHT?
YEP.
SO HE'LL BE BACK.
I'LL GET HIM THEN.
YOU'RE HAPPY ABOUT THAT?
sigh
OH MY GOD!
WHAT THE HELL HAPPENED TO YOU GUYS?
HAVE YOU LOOKED IN A MIRROR?
HUH?
what the heck ...
LET ME GET THIS STRAIGHT.
RATH LET A DEMON GET AWAY?

WELL...
THERE WERE A FEW INTERESTING DEVELOPMENTS.
DEVELOPMENTS?!
GRRRR
hmph
hmph
OOPS
I shouldn't have said anything
WAY TO GO, SLICK.
RATH!
SPIT IT OUT, RATH!
ARE YOU CAUSING PROBLEMS AGAIN?
TELL US WHAT HAPPENED!
PLEASE SAY IT WASN'T A DEMON.
......
YOUR MAJESTY! THIS ISN'T FUNNY! WHY ARE YOU LAUGHING?
I-I-I DON'T KNOW!!!

WELCOME.
MY SINCEREST APOLOGIES FOR DRAGGING YOU OUT HERE.
WHO ARE YOU?
I AM KHARL.
THE ALCHEMIST.

I'VE MADE A MODEST LIFE FOR MYSELF DABBLING IN THINGS DEMONIC.
SURELY YOU'VE HEARD OF ME?
YOU WROTE THE DEMON BIBLE.
AH, DID YOU FIND IT USEFUL? OR, AT THE VERY LEAST, COMP-ELLING?
HMPH.

WHY'D YOU BRING ME HERE?
YOU'RE THE ONLY YOKAI WHO CAN ENTER THE DRAGON CASTLE.
AM I?
YOUR SPOOKY LITTLE TREE STUMP OVER THERE SEEMED TO GET THROUGH EASILY?
I'M HUMAN, NOT YOKAI.
HU-MAN? USING MAGIC?
GARFAKCY USED MAGICAL ASHES THAT I'VE CREATED.
HE WORKS FOR ME.
SO WHAT'S THE FAMOUS ALCHEMIST KHARL DOING THESE DAYS?
STILL MAKING DEMONS?
YOUR REPUTATION PRECEEDS YOU, A MASTER BUILDER OF THE MACABRE, SO TO SPEAK.

THEY WERE BEAUTIFUL ONCE. BUT LEFT BIRD DIED,
AND RIGHT BIRD IS NOT AS ADEPT AT SCULPTING THEIR BRAINS.
IT HAS FORCED ME INTO RETIREMENT.
HOWEVER, YOUR EMERGING ONTO THE SCENE...
HAS GIVEN ME RENEWED INSPIRATION.
YOU'VE BROUGHT ME HERE TO BE AN AUDIENCE FOR YOUR RENEWED INSPIRATION?
NO.

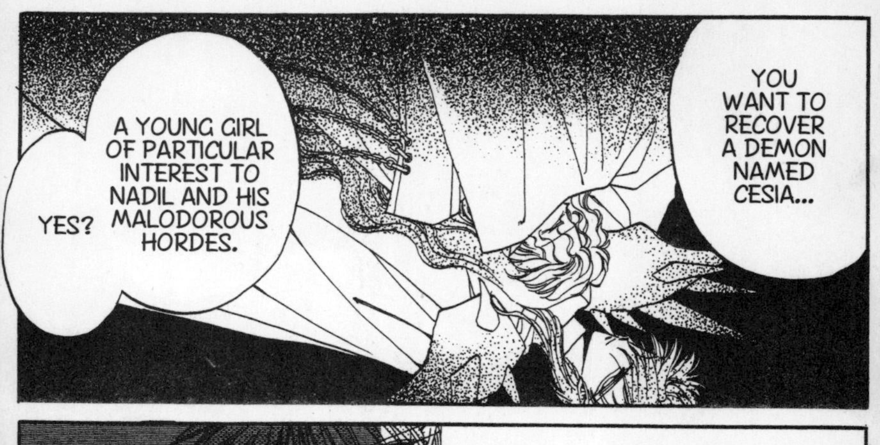

YOU WANT TO RECOVER A DEMON NAMED CESIA...
A YOUNG GIRL OF PARTICULAR INTEREST TO NADIL AND HIS MALODOROUS HORDES.
YES?

I AM SORRY THAT YOU ARE HAVING TROUBLE.

WOULD YOU LIKE MY HELP...

BIERREZ?

GOOD MORNING, CREWGER!

AND DID YOU HAVE A PLEASANT SLEEP?
THERE WAS A LOT OF ACTIVITY LAST NIGHT.
OH.
MORNING, ALL! DORO, TANGY, GUNAN...
Fou, Gran, and...
BREAK-FAST'S HERE!
CESIA?

HEY!
WHERE IS EVERY-ONE?
I BROUGHT FOOD.
thud
UH... GARAVA AND BUBULY?
Shake Shake
NO?
UM,
GEA AND GARLING!
DID I BRING TOO MUCH?
Uh...
REAL-LY?
here
SO ALL THE DARNAS* ARE OUT TODAY,
EH?
riding dragons

?
Aaargh!
thump thump
YOU'RE TAKING CARE OF THE DARNAS, CESIA?
rub rub
YEAH.
THEY NEED ATTENTION.
Wag Wag
chomp chomp
SO, THEY ALL WENT ON A SCOUT MISSION?
THIS MORNING?
splash splash
HUH?

C-
CREWGER TALKS TO YOU?
SURE.
BUT YOU CAN HEAR HIM, TOO.
CAN'T YOU?
I CAN'T.
CAN YOU TALK TO THE DARNAS, AS WELL?
CLUNK
YEAH. BUT THEY HAVE A LIMITED VOCABULARY.
YOU HEAR THEM SPEAK?
?
UH...
WHAT'S THE BIG DEAL?
NEITHER THE LORD NOR RATH CAN HEAR HIM.
TO HAVE THIS GIFT ...
SHE'S LIKE A FAIRY...
SO, IF YOU CAN HEAR CREWGER, YOU MUST ASK HIM SOMETHING.

WHAT?
Only I can hear them?
Why?
flip
THAT'S STRANGE.

WHAT'S WRONG?
THIS REPORT DOESN'T MAKE SENSE...
slap
RUWALK!
YOU GAVE KAI-STERN EXTRA MONEY FOR HIS TRIP!
EVEN AFTER I TOLD YOU NOT TO!
GULP
BUT, THAT WAS A LONG TIME AGO...

HEY.
YOU DO THIS EVERY TIME!
HE'S ONLY SUPPOSED TO GET MONEY FROM ME OR THE LORD!
flip
THIS SCREWS UP THE BUDGET NUMBERS!
Well, don't get mad at me!
flip

WHAT'S UP?
JUST READ-ING.
it's a hobby
flip

AND THEM?
THE SAME OLD STUFF.
ARGUING OVER KAI-STERN'S EXPENSE REPORTS.
what does he need so much cash for?
flip
OKAY.

WHAT?
I JUST SAW HIM COME IN.
HE'S WITH THE LORD.
LOOK AT `EM GO.
they're fast
oh man
KAI-STERN, WHY COULDN'T YOUR TIMING HAVE BEEN BETTER?
GOOD JOB.
HOW'S ZULEBIGGIA?
THAT SILVER-TONGUED MINISTER'S STILL CALLING THE SHOTS.
BUT LIFE WAS PEACEFUL ENOUGH.
THE FISHING INDUSTRY'S DOING WELL, AND...
...?
KAI-STERN!

RATH?
?
?
KAI-STERN! EXPLAIN THE DISPERSION OF FUNDS DURING YOUR TRIP! ANY LEFT?
YOU HAVE TERRIBLE TIMING.
HUH?
ALFEEGI'S GONNA BUST YOUR BALLS.
It's too bad.

THEY WERE BUSINESS EXPENSES.
I SUPPOSE BUSINESS TOOK YOU ON A TOUR OF ZULEBIGGIA'S FINER PUBS?
AND A LONG TOUR, I MIGHT ADD.
FESS UP. HOW MANY TANKARDS DID YOU KNOCK BACK WITH THE LOCAL RABBLE?

HAVE A BIT MORE FAITH IN ME.
really!
Ahem!
I SAW YOU STUMBLE OUT OF LASTILIFUN TAVERN IN ZULEBIGGIA.

T-T-TETHEUS?!
I WAS TRAVELING, TOO.
SO! IS IT TRUE?!

MY LORD!

I SENT KAI-STERN ON A SPECIAL MISSION, ALFEEGI.
GO EASY ON HIM. HE HAD GOOD REASONS FOR EVERYTHING HE DID.
YOU DON'T HAVE TO COVER FOR HIM, YOUR MAJESTY.
DON'T YOU TRUST THE LORD'S JUDGEMENT?!

FINE... I TRUST YOU.
NO, NOT ME. PUT YOUR TRUST IN THE LORD, ALFEEGI.

WHADYA GET ME?
ENOUGH DIRT ON DEMONS TO MAKE YOU SALIVATE.

....
WE SHOULD ALL BE ATTENDING TO MORE SERIOUS MATTERS!
OOOF.
Grab.
He's about to cry.

OH.

WHACK

ばさ!

?

KEEP IT.
A COAT?
MY LORD, I BROUGHT THAT GIRL YOU WANTED BACK WITH ME.
THE ONE FROM THE BAR.
rustle
rustle
OH, HER.
demon info
THANKS FOR HIDING IT IN THE COAT, KAI-STERN.
MY LORD!

I HAVE SOME NEWS.
CAN IT WAIT? I MUST SEE A GUEST.
IT IS URGENT.
A TRAGEDY HAS BEFALLEN THE FAERIE FOREST.
FAERIE FOREST?!
GO ON,
TETHEUS.

WE DON'T HAVE FINAL CONFIRMATION...

BUT EARLY REPORTS SUGGEST THAT ALL LIFE THERE HAS BEEN DESTROYED.

I'M CONCERNED ABOUT AQUITANIA.
WE'VE ALSO RECEIVED IRREGULAR REPORTS FROM OTHER ELFIN GROVES.

MY LORD ...

I'M STARVED.
Chink
Chink
WE GOT GUESTS OR SOMETHING?
FOOd!
YES.
ONE OF THE LORD'S HUMAN FRIENDS IS HERE.
OH.
HUMAN?
MIND IF I TAG ALONG?
OKAY.
BUT THIS FOOD'S NOT FOR YOU, SIR.
WHAT?!
Why doesn't anyone trust me?

PLEASE WAIT RIGHT HERE.
LORD LYKOULEON WILL BE WITH YOU SHORTLY.
SIR THATZ,
MEET ONE OF LORD LYCOULEON'S DEAR FRIENDS, MISS KITCHEL.

K-K-
KITCHEL?!
HUH?
THATZ?! WHAT THE HELL?!!
I KNEW YOU WERE BOTH THIEVES ONCE, BUT...
HE'S A DRAGON KNIGHT? THE WORLD REALLY IS DOOMED.
AND WHAT HAVE YOU DONE RECENTLY FOR THE BENEFIT OF PEACE?
I DIDN'T KNOW YOU KNEW EACH OTHER.
THE LORD GAVE YOU THE RADAR ROCK?
IM-POS-SI-BLE.

OF COURSE HE GAVE IT TO ME.
HOW ELSE WAS I SUPPOSED TO FIND THE MAP PIECES FOR HIM?
DIDN'T YOU KNOW?
NO, I DIDN'T **KNOW.** JUST LIKE YOU DIDN'T **KNOW** ABOUT ME UNTIL JUST NOW EITHER, YOU BACK-STABBING BIT...
ガーっ
YOUR MAJESTY ...
I HAVE ONLY ONE MORE PIECE TO FIND. BUT I'LL NEED THE OTHERS TO CONTINUE.
YOU'VE FOUND ALL OF THEM?
YES!
AND I'M ONLY A STEP AWAY FROM FINDING THE THREE TREASURES FOR YOU!

IT WON'T BE THAT SIMPLE.
OH, PLEASE.
I'M A THIEF, EVERY-THING'S SIMPLE.
he's pisse
crush
THE DEMONS HAVE SEEPED FURTHER INTO THE PEACEFUL LANDS, KITCHEL.
YOU'VE BEEN VERY LUCKY SO FAR.
THATZ.
YES, MY LORD?

I WOULD LIKE YOU TO ACCOM-PANY KITCHEL...
AND FIND THE THREE TREASURES.

WHAT?!

NO WAY!!
I'M NOT GOING ANY-WHERE WITH THIS PICK-POCKET!!
ガターン!
I CAN'T LET THATZ COME WITH ME!
HE'LL GOUGE ME FOR EVERY-THING I HAVE AND LEAVE ME STRANDED AND SOME...!
SHE STOLE MY MONEY AND LEFT ME STRANDED!
I DON'T TRUST THIS LIAR ANY MORE THAN SHE CAN THROW ME!
I DON'T NEED HELP!
AND, LORD!
WHAT IF BIERREZ COMES BACK?
YOU'LL NEED ME HERE!
KITCHEL.
you'll probably run into demons.
THE TASK IS DANGER-OUS. I MUST SEND A DRAGON KNIGHT WITH YOU.

WELL ...
But Thatz?
THATZ.
I KNOW, I KNOW.
RUNE AND I ARE USELESS AGAINST BIERREZ.
BUT WHY NOT SEND RUNE?
HE CAN DEAL WITH THAT WOMAN.
"THAT WO-MAN"?
.....
NO.
I MUST SEND RUNE ON ANOTHER MISSION.

I LOST TRACK OF TIME FEEDING THE DARNAS.
I BETTER HURRY.
it's night already
GEEZ, CESIA DOES THIS EVERY DAY.
IT PUZZLES ME WHY SHE FEELS IT NECESSARY TO HIDE IT FROM ALL OF US.

!

KAI-STERN?

HELLO.

oh...

I DIDN'T KNOW YOU WERE BACK.

DOES RATH TELL YOU EVERYTHING?
WHY DO YOU ASK?
BECAUSE YOU'RE HIS CLOSEST FRIEND.
NO.
hee hee
I WISH WHAT YOU SAID WERE TRUE,
BUT RATH HATES ME.
HATES YOU?
WHY?
YOU'LL FIND OUT SOME-DAY.
RATH KEEPS IT FROM YOU AND THATZ.
HE CARES DEEPLY ABOUT THE TWO OF YOU.
WHAT?!
THATZ IS...

...GOING WITH KITCHEL TO FIND MAP PIECES?!
THAT'S RIGHT.
HI! ♪
DID YOU ARRIVE YESTER-DAY?
YEP.
THAT GUY WITH WHITE HAIR SHOWED ME IN.
I CAN HANDLE THE JOB ALONE, BUT THE LORD INSISTS THAT THATZ TAG ALONG.
KINDA LIKE MY LITTLE PUPPY DOG.
ha
ha
.....
slurp
MAN! I WANNA GO DEMON-HUNTING!
WE KNOW YOU WANT TO GO DEMON-HUNTING!!
jealous
jealous
jealous

WHEN DO YOU LEAVE?

IT'S UP TO KAI-STERN.

WE'RE LEAVING TOGETHER.

READY, THATZ?

YOU DONE EATING?

WHAT? ALREADY?

HE'S ALWAYS RUSHING AWAY, ISN'T HE?
RUNE?
THE LORD WANTS TO SPEAK WITH YOU.
...THE FAERIE FOREST?

YOUR ARM...
IT'S NOT YOURS
YOU ATTACHED SOMEONE ELSE'S TO REPLACE YOUR OWN.
RATH CUT MINE OFF A LONG TIME AGO.
A GOOD FRIEND SACRIFICED HIS LIFE TO GIVE ME THIS.

THE FAERIE FOREST IS DEAD?
DID THE MONSTER FISH VARAWOO KILL IT?
WHAT ABOUT THE WATER LIGHTS?
AND SO IS ...
...TINTLET?
YOU LEAVING, TOO, RUNE?

RATH ...
I'M SORRY.
I WANTED TO STAY AND HELP YOU DEFEND THE CASTLE AGAINST BIERREZ.
BUT I'M WORRIED ABOUT THE FAERIE FOREST.
NO SWEAT.
LIKE I'M COMPLAINING? HEY, MORE BIERREZ ASS-KICKING FOR ME.
UM ... ER ...
you better run along now
HE MAKES ME NERVOUS.
WELL ...
BEFORE I GO...

RATH!
ARE YOU HIDING SOMETHING FROM THATZ AND ME?
YES I AM.
......
that was easy
Pi
Pi
Pi
Pi
Pi
Pi
WHY DO YOU ALWAYS ...
HUH?
WHAT?
squeeze
......

BECAUSE HE CARES DEEPLY ABOUT YOU TWO.
IT'S OKAY.
YOU CAN TELL ME SOME OTHER TIME.
RATH.
......
I CAN'T, RUNE.
I DON'T WANT YOU TO KNOW, EVER. THAT'S WHY I MUST KILL BIERREZ.
BIERREZ KNOWS WHO I TRULY AM. AND THE SECRET WILL DIE WITH HIM.

fizz
fizz
!
さら....

WHAT YOU DO?
CAST A SLEEP SPELL WITH MASTER KHARL'S MAGIC DUST.
IT WILL HAVE NO AFFECT ON DEMONS, BUT WILL SEND THE DRAGON TRIBE AND ITS BROOD INTO SWEET SOMNO-LENCE.
I DIDN'T ASK YOU TO DO THAT!
NO, BUT MASTER KHARL DID.
I'LL DO MY THING AND YOU DO YOURS.
HERE. YOU CAN WAKE HIM UP WITH THAT, IF YOU WANT.
?
BUT I'D KILL RATH WHILE HE'S ASLEEP.
IT'D PROVE THE EFFICACY OF MASTER KHARL'S EXPERIMENT IF YOU EXTIN-GUISH RATH'S FLAME IN THE THROES OF HIS DREAMS.

RATH WILL NOT SUCCOMB TO A SIMPLE SLEEP SPELL!

OH.
THEN I WISH YOU LUCK. AND MAY THE ARM THAT MASTER KHARL MADE STRONGER FOR YOU BRING YOU VICTORY AGAINST THE DRAGON KNIGHT.
step
BUT DON'T GET YOURSELF KILLED. WE NEED THE INFORMATION YOU BRING BACK.

I see.

heh

Hmpf!

This arm is just an experiment to him.

bink

I ALREADY TOLD RATH ABOUT CESIA'S POWER.
IT DOESN'T MATTER.
I'LL BE A GUINEA PIG.
AS LONG AS IT STOPS RATH FROM DOING TO CESIA...
...WHAT HE DID TO ME!

OW ...

THE AIR'S POLLUTED...
SOME-ONE'S CAST A SLEEP SPELL OVER EVERY-ONE.
THE DRAGON TRIBE IS VULNER-ABLE.
THUMP
THUMP
AM I ...
...THE ONLY ONE STILL AWAKE?

IS IT BIER-REZ?
OR ANOTHER YOKAI?

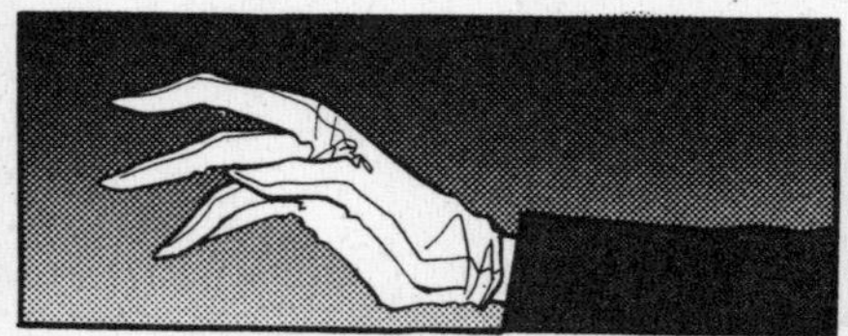

CESIA?
......
!!!
WHAAAAA!
HUH?
HEY!
TETH-EUS?!
WHAT'S GOING ON?
IS THIS THE WORK OF DEMON MAGIC?
IT'S A SLEEP SPELL. IT AFFECTS EVERYONE EXCEPT FOR YOKAI. SO I'M FINE.
ARE YOU OKAY?
He should be asleep.
I AM THE DRAGON TRIBE SECRUITY OFFICER. I MUST SECURE THE CASTLE.
WHAT ?!!

A DEMON DID THIS.

IT'S AFTER EITHER NADIL'S HEAD, OR THE LORD HIMSELF.

I'M IM-PRESSED.

......

OR CESIA ...

hmmm

PLEASE, GO AND PROTECT THEM!

Uh... Tetheus?

HMMM ......

WE PROMISED TO PROTECT YOU.

WHAT?

SO ME MUSN'T SEPARATE.

WE CAN BOTH CHECK ON THE LORD.

OKAY ...

he's weird

HEY!
FREAK!

YOU PERFORMED THAT SLEEP SPELL WITH APLOMB.
BUT YOU DIDN'T REALLY THINK IT WOULD AFFECT ME.
SO, I ONLY ASSUME YOU CAST IT AS A WAY TO MANAGE US BEING ALONE. I THOUGHT I'D OBLIGE.
NAH.
I JUST WANTED TO KILL YOU...
...WITHOUT ANY INTERRUPTIONS.
BESIDES, NOW YOU CAN FIGHT ME IN YOUR TRUE FORM RATHER THAN IN THIS RIDICULOUS SHELL. IT'S HARDLY BECOMING OF YOU.
IS THAT WHAT YOU WANT?

AND THIS TIME ...
YOU WON'T CATCH ME OFF GUARD!

!!
UGH!
WHAT THE HELL?

I CAN'T MOVE! I'M PAR-ALYZED

I HAVE T ADMIR YOUR HIGH THRESH OLD FO PAIN.
OF COURSE, IF YOU HAD JUST ANSWERED MY QUESTION EARLIER...
WE COULD HAVE AVOIDED THIS UNFORTUNATE BLOODLETTING.
UGH ...
cough
BUT THANK YOU FOR YOUR ANSWER. NOW GO BACK TO SLEEP.
......
SWEET DREAMS, RUWALK.
NOW ...

THERE'S A SEVERED HEAD LYING ABOUT THAT I MUST BRING BACK TO MASTER KHARL. WHERE COULD IT BE?
WHAT THE...
I'M NUMB...
WELL ...
KHARL'S POISON HAS GIVEN ME A DISTINCT ADVANTAGE OVER YOU.

KHARL?
crackle
IT'S A SHAME THAT I'M GOING TO KILL YOU...
...BEFORE YOU'VE HAD A CHANCE TO DEVELOP AN IMMUNITY TO IT!
!!

ZOMA!!
IMPOS-SIBLE!
YOUR LEGS...
YOU'RE STAND-ING...
WITH-OUT YOUR BIRD... HOW?
STAND DOWN.
I WON'T LET YOU KILL RATH.

REMOVE THE PARALY-SIS FROM HIS BODY AND BACK OFF.
I DON'T BELIEVE THIS.
cough
AS LONG AS I'M HERE, I WILL NOT ALLOW YOU TO HARM,
RATH OR CESIA!
ZOMA!!

PROTECTED BEHIND A BATTERY OF DRAGON OFFICER SPELLS, EH?
THIS COULD BE TOUGH.
BUT THE RED OFFICER'S SPELL IS MISSING.
SO I'LL START THERE.

SO, YOU WANT TO STEAL NADIL'S HEAD.
CLICK

BUT YOU'RE NOT IN NADIL'S ARMY. SO, WHAT WOULD YOU WANT WITH IT?

CESIA!
WHERE ARE YOU?
I HOPE SHE'S NOT ALONE ...

Shhh
!
pant
pant
CREWGER!

......

THE DRAGON TRIBE IS SHORT-SIGHTED. THEY SHOULDN'T LOCK NADIL'S HEAD AWAY...

THEY SHOULD PUT IT TO USE.

YOU AGREE?

THE POSSIBILITIES ARE LIMITLESS, YOKAI PRINCESS.
MR. KHARL CAN REVIVE NADIL, EASILY.
YOU CAN BE A PART OF IT, TOO. I'LL TAKE YOU TO HIM.
YOU'RE A FOOL!
......
HUH?
THE LAST THING I WANT TO SEE IS THAT ODIOUS TYRANT REVIVED AND SET LOOSE TO ENSLAVE EVEN MORE PEOPLES.
THE FACT THAT I'M A YOKAI DOESN'T MATTER IN THE SLIGHTEST.
I HATE NADIL!
OKAY?!

I'M GLAD THERE'S NOTHING LEFT OF HIM...
BUT HIS ROTTING HEAD!
IS SHE HIDING SOMETHING?
BUT YOU CANNOT DENY YOUR BLOOD. YOU **ARE** A YOKAI.
WHY ARE YOU SIDING WITH THE DRAGON TRIBE WHOSE AIM IS TO ERADICATE YOUR PEOPLE?
SPARE ME.
YOU'RE A HUMAN SIDING WITH NADIL.
LEAVE HERE NOW!
HMPH.
AND I SUPPOSE IF I **DON'T**, YOU'LL CALL FOR HELP.
OR WILL YOU TAKE IT UPON YOURSELF TO CAST ME OUT.
TRY ME.

HEH-HEH...

?

HA, HA, HA!

HA!

......
STEP ASIDE ZOMA.
I DON'T WANT TO HURT YOU.
I'M ONLY AFTER RATH.
OH, I'M NOT GOOD ENOUGH TO FIGHT?
RATH!
ZOMA...
I'M FINE.
MY BODY IS ADAPTING TO THE POISON.
COME ON, BIERREZ.
LET'S GO.

!
HUH!?
!
THAT'S ...
CESIA'S WIND?!
!
WHAT'S GARFAKCY DOING?!

UGH!
I CAN'T COMPLETELY CONTROL MY POWERS!
I HAVE TO AVOID HARMING THE CASTLE!

BANG
!!
HER STRENGTH ...
snap
... IT SURPASSES THAT OF THE YOKAI!
SUCH STRANGE POWER!
float

THAT'S WHY SHE'S NADIL'S FAVORITE, GARFAKCY.
Flutter
!

......

AREN'T YOU THE LEAST BIT CURIOUS?

DON'T YOU WANT TO LEARN THE SECRET BEHIND THIS PHENOMENAL POWER OF HERS?

NADIL HID HER FOR GOOD REASON, YES?

KHARL!
SHE'S THE ONE WE NEED.

BRING HER TO ME DEAD OR ALIVE. I CAN ALWAYS REVIVE HER.

LET THE DRAGON KNIGHTS TEAR BIERREZ APART.

!
fwoosh
CESIA'S FIGHT-ING!
BUT WHO?!
!
Zip!
WHERE YOU GOING?
WE'LL SETTLE THIS LATER!
clang
I TRUST NEITHER OF US WANT THEM TO STEAL AWAY WITH CESIA, RIGHT?
!
......
rat-at-at
She's strong...
I CAN KILL HER, EH?

I'LL DO IT!
SWALLOW A DEATH SEED, YOKAI!
SWISH
?!
TSK!
CREWGER!!

CREWGER?
CREWGER!
NO!
Uhhh
NO.
NO.
...
.....
OH,
NO...
SOB

YOU FOUL HUMAN!
WHAT ARE YOU AFTER?!
IT'S NOT JUST NADIL'S HEAD THAT BROUGHT YOU HERE?!

MY MASTER, KHARL THE ALCHEMIST ...
WANTS YOU... **DEAD** OR ALIVE... PRINCESS.
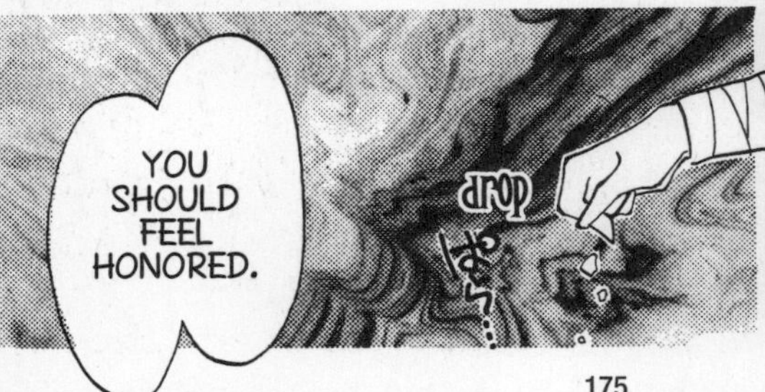
YOU SHOULD FEEL HONORED.
drop

!!

ズボッ

!

AARRGHH!!

YOU ... WON'T ...

TAKE ... ME ... AWAY!

ゆら…

thWack
!!
GAR-FAKCY!!
!
WHAT ARE YOU DOING TO CESIA?!
BIERREZ!
WHAT HAVEN'T YOU DONE TO RATH?! HE SHOULD BE DEAD.
faint
OH ...
RATH!!
OH, RATH!
RATH!!

I...
I LET CREW-GER DIE!
I'M SORRY!!
IT'S OKAY.
I KNEW HE'D DO THIS SOME-DAY.
plop
plop
IT'S...
IT'S MY FAULT.
thump
thump
RATH?
WELL, BIER-REZ. WERE YOU ABLE TO WORK OUT YOUR DIFFERENCES WITH THE OBJECT OF YOUR SCORN?
OR DID RATH BEAT YOU?
I'LL KILL RATH LATER.
NOW, I WANT TO KNOW WHAT YOU WANT WITH CESIA.
ガッ
MASTER KHARL HAS CHANGED HIS MIND.

ZZZT
YES.
NADIL'S HEAD INTRIGUES ME.
BUT NOT NEARLY AS MUCH AS THE GIRL'S POWER.
I WANT HER.
KHARL!
KHARL!

?!
ARGHHHHHHH!
WHAT THE...?
I'VE RIDDLED YOUR ARM...
... WITH SO MUCH POISON AND DEMON SEED...
BIERREZ ...
CLICK
BLURB
BLURB
YOU ARE NOW MINE, MIND, BODY AND SOUL.
KILL...
...CESIA!

!
HUH?
BIERREZ! GET HER! I'VE PARALYZED RATH, AGAIN!
BIERREZ! DON'T!
UGH ...
BIER ...
......
BIERREZ! LET GO OF HER!
UNNNH

BIERREZ! THAT'S CESIA!
CESIA, BIERREZ!!
IT'S NO USE.
MASTER KHARL CONTROLS HIM NOW.
ZOMA?
BIERREZ!
YOU'RE GOING TO KILL CESIA!
IT'S CESIA!
CESIA?!
thump
thump

MENU
HE LET HER GO?!
THAT'S IMPOSSIBLE!
RAA... TH...
YOU MUST...
KILL...
ME...!
CESIA?!
I CAN'T FIGHT THIS POSESSION!

I'M BECOMING A MONSTER.
A MONSTER LIKE ME SHOULD DIE...
I...
...AGREE.
BUT... DON'T... HURT HER...
CESIA...
SHE HAS GREAT POWER.
YOU NEED HER POWER.

YES.
I SUP-POSE SO.

I WASN'T GOING TO GIVE HER TO NADIL'S ARMY.
thump
thump
YOU MUST BELIEVE HAT ALL I EVER VANTED TO DO WAS ROTECT CESIA.

I DON'T CARE WHAT HAPPENS TO ME.

BUT ...

I JUST CAN'T ...

... KILL HER.

ZOMA!

!

GET THAT HUMAN KID OUTTA HERE.

Uhh...

YOU GOT IT!

KHARL!

COME BACK,

GAR-FAKCY!

buzz

yank

NADIL'S SPELL DISGUISED YOU AS A HUMAN THEN.
BUT EVEN IF YOU HAD BEEN A HUMAN,
I STILL WOULD HAVE...
MENU

MOUNT
MFARTHA?

THE WITCH TOLD ME ONCE
THAT MT. MFARTHA'S LEGENDARY BEAST CAN RESURRECT THE DEAD.
I'D
LIKE TO REVIVE
CREW-GER!
I'VE NEVER HEARD THAT STORY.
NADIL'S ARMY KEEPS IT A SECRET.
ONLY A FEW YOKAI KNOW.
IT'S TOO DANGEROUS A JOURNEY FOR YOU TO EMBARK UPON.
I'LL SEND SOME-ONE ELSE.
NO!
I MUST GO.

YOU ARE FREE TO MAKE YOUR OWN DECISIONS, CESIA.
THANK YOU, SIRE!
BE CARE-FUL.
MAN.
...
CAN I GO HUNT DEMONS, TOO?
NO!
all alone
erck
erck
SIR ...
......
hey look
CAN'T I GO WITH HER?
could be a lot of demons
snap
WE SAID, NO!
snap
snap

I'M SUR-PRISED YOU LET CESIA GO.
....
WHY WOULDN'T I?
YOU'VE KNOWN ABOUT HER POWER ALL ALONG.
AH. SO RATH, YOU ASSUMED...
THAT I HAVE NO PLANS TO USE HER FOR OUR PURPOSES.
CAN'T YOU TRUST ME...
RATH?
!!

I HATE IT WHEN YOU CODDLE ME.
AND CONDE-SCEND TO ME!
I'M NOT YOUR TOY!

RATH!

I'LL BE GONE FOR AWHILE.
THANKS FOR RETURNING TO FULFILL MY DUTIES, SARAZAR.
BOW

SORRY TO DISTURB YOUR ETERNAL REST.
IT'S OK.

I OWE MUCH TO THE DRAGON TRIBE.

SO ...
YOU'RE GOING TO MT. MFARTHA?
YES.
MY MIND'S MADE UP.

IT'S VERY FAR NORTH.
NOT EVEN THE CRYSTAL CAN SEE THAT FAR.
AND A LARGE, DREADFUL MONSTER LIVES THERE.
MUST YOU GO?

I HAVE TO!
I OWE HIM.

AFTER I LEARN HOW TO BRING CREWGER BACK TO LIFE, I'LL DO THE SAME FOR YOU!
YOU DON'T HAVE TO DO THAT.
oh, but I will

BUT, CESIA...
DO NOT FORGET...

SOON YOU WILL LEARN YOUR DESTINY...
AND IT MAY LEAD THE WORLD TO RUIN.
HOW-EVER...
YOUR DESTINY ALSO HOLDS THE KEY TO SAVING THE WORLD.
PHEW!
I CAN BREATHE! ♪

LET'S SEE...
THUD!
rustle
rustle
.....
.....
HEY.
WHAT THE HELL ARE YOU DOING HERE?!
HEH-HEH, HEH
I THOUGHT YOU COULDN'T ABANDON THE CASTLE!
I FELT THE NEED TO KICK SOME SERIOUS DEMON BUTT...
...SO I GOT A STAND-IN.
STAND-IN?!
WHO?

A FRIEND.
HE OWES ME.
WHERE'S RATH?
QUIETLY STARING OUT THE WINDOW.
creak
......
slam
WEIRD. KEEP AN EYE ON HIM.
Whew.
しーん
THEY ARE GONE.
DARN IT!
WHY'S RATH SO RECK-LESS?!
they'll find out
UH-HUH
HE LEFT FIRE BEHIND!

MAYBE HE GAVE ME LEGS...
SO HE COULD MAKE ME DO THIS FOR HIM.
I feel tricked
YOU'RE RIGHT
RATH?
CAN I COME IN?
KNOCK
KNOCK
QUICK! THE TRANSFOR -MING PLANT!
UH-OH
SO, WHO'S COVERING FOR YOU?
LOOK! A STAR!
I CAN'T TELL HER ...
FORGET THE STAR.
TELL ME WHO!
DRAGON KNIGHTS 4 • THE END

Dragon Knights

Preview for Volume 5:

The Dragon Knights have been dispatched again in the service of the Dragon Lord, but this time to three different corners of the realm. Thatz, reluctantly reunited with Kitche, journeys to find the three treasures. Rath, reluctantly gaurding Cesia, travels to Mt. Mfartha. And Rune, having regained his elfin powers, heads toward the Faerie Forest, concerned for his brethren. The battle to save the peaceful lands is looking grim, and with Kharl the Alchemist vying for the power of both Cesia and Nadil, the Dragon Tribe is taking a risk spreading its forces thin, especially with reports of demon forces closing in on them from all sides.

Mineko Ohkami

5

STOP!

This is the back of the book.
ou wouldn't want to spoil a great ending!

This book is printed "manga-style," in the authentic Japanese right-to-left format. Since none of the artwork has been flipped or altered, readers get to experience the story just as the creator intended. You've been asking for it, so TOKYOPOP® delivered: authentic, hot-off-the-press, and far more fun!

DIRECTIONS

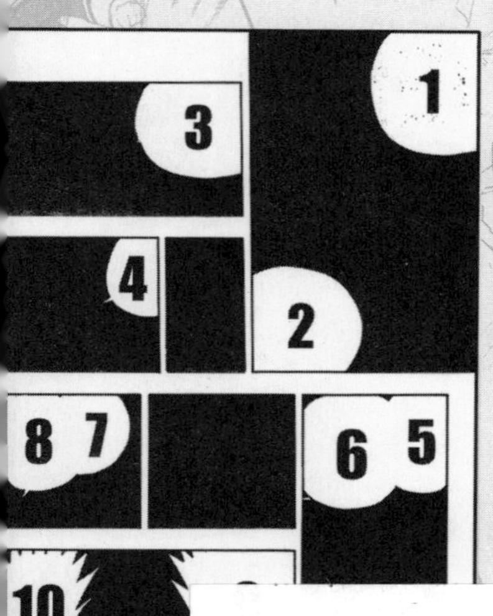

If this is your first time reading manga-style, here's a quick guide to help you understand how it works.

It's easy... just start in the top right panel and follow the numbers. Have fun, and look for more 100% authentic manga from TOKYOPOP®!